Cleveland Whitworth bros.

Columbian cook and recipe book

Cleveland Whitworth bros.

Columbian cook and recipe book

ISBN/EAN: 9783744788939

Printed in Europe, USA, Canada, Australia, Japan

Cover: Foto ©Lupo / pixelio.de

More available books at **www.hansebooks.com**

COLUMBIAN

COOK AND RECIPE BOOK,

FOR MAKING

FINE FRENCH FRUIT CREAMS

AND OTHER

CANDIES AND FROSTINGS

AT HOME.

PRICE, - - - 50 CENTS.

CLEVELAND, OHIO.
WHITWORTH BROS., PUBLISHERS,
1893.

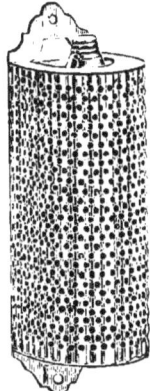

A WORD OF WARNING.

There is a tragic list of diseases which woman alone may suffer from. Men have their physical distresses, but a man is seldom called upon to endure anything so painful, so lingering and tenacious as these diseases to which woman is peculiarly subjected, and which are especially terrible, for the reason that most of them effect the mind as well as the body.

They induce irritability, they destroy ambition, and they injure the memory. Ninety-nine out of a hundred women are afflicted with some of these complaints in a greater or less degree, and so used have they become to pain that they can hardly fancy mortal existence without it. Many of them are women of natural brilliancy, and their possibilities for usefulness would be very great if they were not handicapped by these tormenting troubles.

Women have a way of taking their complaints too much as a matter of course. They say, "Every woman has some trouble, I suppose I ought not to complain." And they thus permit a disease to continue until it absorbs the muscular strength, impoverishes the blood, destroys the beauty, sucks up the mental activity, and leaves the victim a pessimistic, faded inadequate, with a hold upon the pity of those about her, but none upon their admiration.

The expense of calling for the treatment of a physician hinders many women from attending to themselves. They do not wish to be an expense to their husbands or fathers, and conceal the suffering until they are almost beyond help. Many young women hesitate to go to a physician because of false modesty. Many have a foolish idea that they will get better after a little while. This is a mistake. The relaxed muscles, the diseased nervous system, and the impoverished blood, are not likely to get back to their normal condition without aid.

VIAVI is the name of a remedy which cures the diseases to which woman is subject. This statement may well be doubted in light of almost complete failure with ordinary methods. Still, we may be right; women who have doctored for many years without success say we are. Others never were well until they used VIAVI. Nearly 100,000 women owe their recovery to VIAVI.

Send two-cent stamp to the office of the VIAVI Company, No. 815 The Cuyahoga, Cleveland, Ohio, for 40 page Health Book to Mothers and Daughters. A direct talk however, is more satisfying. Call during the office hours, (2 to 5 p. m.,) and learn what you may expect from this reform method of treatment.

Every woman bears a great responsibility. She must preserve her own health that she may give a heritage of health to her children. Therefore let her take her ailments in time. If she does not do so, barreness, insanity, or a life of terrible physical torment may be her portion. Remember disease is never the will of God. It does not happen. It is caused. Avoid the cause ; cure it if you can not.

PREFACE.

The price, "forty to eighty cents per pound," for French Cream Candy, makes it a luxury seldom indulged in by people in ordinary circumstances, and the making of them at home is so often attended with failure, that when success does come, the cost, not counting worry and labor, is fully as much as when purchased at the confectioners; and in almost every case the unsightliness of the candy is a source of disappointment. By our process no one need fear a failure in making Fruit Cream Candy or Frosting. The use of Cream gives to them a smoothness and richness attained by no other goods, while for purity and deliciousness of flavor the delicate Fruit Creams surpass all cooked Frostings or Candies. They are perfectly pure, a fact not to be overlooked, and can be made as beautiful, both in shape and color, as in any other manner. The cost of Fruit Creams "eight to fifteen cents per pound," is so low as to place them within the reach of all. The process of making is so simple none need go wrong, and the work is rather a pleasure than labor.

UNCOOKED CANDIES.

INSTRUCTIONS.

Read the following instructions carefully and you will not have the least trouble in making beautiful candy from any of the recipes.

The plain French Cream, or any of the Fruit Cream recipes, will make about one pound of candy.

Cold boiled milk, with one teaspoonful glycerine to cup of milk, will answer in place of cream.

VARIETIES.

An endless variety of candy can be made by moulding with the fingers into different shapes, or pressed with the hand, or rolled with a rolling-pin into sheets and cut into square sticks, etc., or by rolling small balls; lay them on plates and press into buttons or small cakes.

COLORS.

It is not necessary to color any of the Fruit Creams, as the natural color is as fine as can be obtained artificially. Orange gives a handsome orange or yellow, peach a beautiful cream tint; red currant gives nice shade of pink, etc., etc.

Colors can be obtained at any drug store.

Liquid Cochineal will give any shade from most delicate pink to deep red.

Tincture Tumeric, a beautiful yellow.

Burnt sugar or Caramel, any shade of brown.

These, with the different shades of color from the fruits will give a combination of colors to suit the most fastidious.

Confectioners sugar must be used in making all the Fruit Cream Candy and Icing. It is purer than ordinary pulverized sugar, and can be obtained at any leading grocery store.

FRUIT CREAMS.

PEACH CREAMS.

Select a juicy peach, remove the skin and put meat of peach in a bowl ; mash and add two tablespoonfuls sweet cream ; stir in confectioners sugar until perfectly smooth and stiff enough to mould in your hands. Form into desired shapes and lay on marble slab, plates or waxed paper to harden.

BANANA CREAMS.

Mash the fruit in bowl leaving out the center or seed part, add two tablespoonfuls sweet cream and proceed as in peach cream.

ORANGE CREAMS.

Grate the rind and add the juice of orange ; stir in confectioners sugar until quite thick ; add two tablespoonfuls sweet cream, then stir in sugar until stiff enough to mould.

LEMON CREAMS.

Use the juice and grated rind of one lemon ; add one-half teaspoonful glycerine. Stir in confectioners sugar until stiff enough to mould.

STRAWBERRY CREAMS.

One-half cup strawberry juice ; stir in confectioners sugar until quite thick ; add two tablespoonfuls sweet cream. Stir in sugar until stiff enough to mould.

GRAPE CREAMS.

One-half cup grape juice; stir in confectioners sugar until quite thick; add two teaspoonfuls sweet cream. Stir in sugar until stiff enough to mould.

COFFEE CREAMS.

One-half cup strong coffee, three tablespoonfuls sweet cream; stir in confectioners sugar until stiff enough to mould.

PINEAPPLE CREAMS.

Pare and slice pineapple; put in basin with a little sugar and water; place basin in pan of boiling water until juice is extracted; use one-half cup of this syrup with two tablespoonfuls sweet cream. Stir in confectioners sugar until stiff enough to mould.

WINE CREAMS.

One-half cup claret wine; stir in confectioners sugar until quite thick; add three tablespoonfuls sweet cream. Stir in sugar until thick enough to mould.

Malaga, Port, Currant or any other wine may be used in the same manner.

FIG CREAMS.

Three nice fresh figs, cooked with a little water and sugar until the skin can be rubbed smooth; add three tablespoonfuls sweet cream; stir in confectioners sugar until stiff enough to mould. Roll in confectioners sugar after being formed.

PLAIN FRENCH CREAMS.

Half cup sweet cream; stir in confectioners sugar until stiff enough to mould. Flavor with vanilla, almond, lemon, rose or any desired flavor; leave white or color to suit.

CREAM DATES.

Select perfect dates, split and remove pits. Make oblong pieces of any of the foregoing creams, press half of date on each side of cream and mould cream smooth on each side of date.

WINTERGREEN CREAMS.

Make plain French Creams; color pink if desired; flavor with wintergreen and press into round buttons.

NUT CREAMS.

Make plain French Creams; stir in chopped nuts before sugar is all rubbed in; press into sheets, cut in squares or sticks.

PLAIN CHOCOLATE CREAMS.

Make plain French Creams; stir in desired quantity grated chocolate before sugar is all rubbed in. This is nice in squares or sticks, or as walnut creams.

FIG CREAMS.

Select nice layer figs, cut in half and split; make oblong pieces of any of the foregoing creams and press fig around cream the same as with cream dates.

PEPPERMINT CREAMS.

Make plain French Cream; flavor quite strong with peppermint, press into round buttons of desired size.

MAPLE SUGAR CREAMS.

Make plain French Cream; stir in grated maple sugar to taste before confectioners sugar is all rubbed in. This cream is nice cut in squares, or rolled in balls and walnut meats pressed in sides.

FRUIT CREAMS.

Make plain French Creams; add dates, figs, citron and seeded raisins chopped fine; mixed in before the sugar is all rubbed in. Make into sheet half inch thick by pressing with hand or rolling out with rolling pin. Cut into squares or sticks or mould into any shape, and cover with chocolate, as Chocolate Creams.

COCOANUT CREAMS.

Make plain French Creams; stir in grated cocoanut before sugar is all rubbed in. Roll into sheet and cut into squares or sticks or press into round cakes. This cream is pretty colored pink with cochineal, or brown with grated chocolate.

WALNUT CREAMS.

Take plain French Creams or any of the Fruit Creams; roll in ball nearly one inch in diameter; press half walnut meat into one or both sides, and lay on plate or waxed paper to harden.

VARIEGATED CREAM ROLL.

Take three or four different colored creams, make into roll six or eight inches long, with the colors well-mixed. Make sheet of plain chocolate cream one-quarter inch thick, six or eight inches wide to suit length of roll, and about seven inches long ; roll this entirely around roll already formed, lay on waxed paper to harden ; turn it occasionally to keep in shape. This is a very handsome candy and will remain soft and creamy for months, so as to slice like cake, "if you can keep it that long."

CITRON CREAMS.

Make ball of vanilla or any of the Fruit Creams, cut very small pieces of citron, press on top of ball; set on plates or waxed paper to harden.

PECAN OR HICKORYNUT CREAMS.

Make balls of vanilla or any of the fruit creams; press pecan or hickorynut meats into one or both sides ball; lay on waxed paper to harden.

VARIEGATED CREAMS.

Take three or four different colored creams ; twist into roll so the colors will be mixed ; form into buttons, squares or cubes, or roll into balls and press walnut meats into sides. Beautiful candies can be made in this way.

FRENCH CHOCOLATE CREAMS.

Use any of the foregoing creams ; form into desired shapes ; lay on plate or waxed papers to dry ; melt chocolate by putting confectioners chocolate in bowl ; place bowl in basin of boiling water until chocolate melts, or set bowl in oven. Be careful in either case not to cook the chocolate. When cream is hard enough to handle, place one at a time on a fork and dip in chocolate until entirely covered ; scrape dripping chocolate off bottom of fork on side of bowl ; slip covered cream onto waxed paper to harden. Orange, Peach, Strawberry, Vanilla or Wine Creams are very delicious.

NEAPOLITAN CREAMS.

Press plain French Cream into sheet half inch thick, same with pink Cocoanut, Orange and plain Chocolate Creams ; lay cocoanut sheet on plain cream, orange on cocoanut and chocolate on orange, press together and cut into squares, or as desired. What is cut from edges may be rolled into balls, making beautiful, variegated creams.

ALMOND CREAMS.

Make a ball of French Cream or any of the Fruit Creams; press almond into side edgewise leaving about half of almond out; lay on waxed paper to harden.

RAISIN CREAMS.

Select extra sized raisins, split and remove seeds; make small, oblong pieces vanilla or Fruit Creams; wrap raisin around cream same as Date Creams. This makes nice dainty candies.

FILBERT CREAMS.

Make ball of vanilla or any of the Fruit Creams; press filbert meat into ball leaving half nut out; lay on waxed paper to harden. Filberts make one of the prettiest nut candies.

CREAM BON-BON

Make a roll one and a quarter inch in diameter and about three inches long, of two or more colored creams, delicate shades are best. With case knife scrape side of roll just enough to fur it. Cut slice length of roll and nearly quarter inch thick, twist this into open spiral, double ends together and form into round bon-bon, with furred side on top. Two or three trials and you will succeed; there will be no loss, as you can work it over if not successful first time. No handsomer candies are made than these.

COOKED CANDIES.

- -

POP CORN BALLS.

One cup white sugar, water enough to dissolve it; boil until syrup will thread; put pop corn in a pan and pour candy over it. Make into balls.

MOLASSES CANDY.

One cup of molasses, one cup of sugar, butter the size of an egg, one tablespoonful vinegar; boil, but do not stir, until it hardens when dropped into cold water. When done stir in a teaspoonful of soda; pour into buttered pans; flavor to suit; when cool pull until white.

HOARHOUND CANDY.

Boil two ounces dried hoarhound in a pint and a half of water for half an hour; strain and add three and a half pounds sugar; boil until hard when dropped in cold water; pour into greased tins; when cold mark into sticks or squares.

HICKORYNUT CANDY.

Two cups sugar, half cup water; boil without stirring until hard. Flavor to taste, then stir in one cup of nuts; pour on buttered plates and cut in squares.

ICE CREAM CANDY.

Three cups of sugar, one-half cup of vinegar, cup and a half of water, butter size of walnut. Flavor to taste. Boil until hard; pull white.

CHOCOLATE CARAMELS.

Two cups of molasses, one cup of brown sugar, one cup milk, half pound chocolate, butter size of egg; beat all together; boil until hard when dropped into water; turn into greased pans. When nearly cold cut into small squares.

BUTTER SCOTCH.

Three pounds coffee sugar, one-quarter pound butter; add sufficient water only to dissolve the sugar; boil without stirring until it will easily break when dropped in cold water. When done add one-half teaspoonful cream tartar and flavor to taste; pour into greased tins and when partly cold mark off into small squares.

FIG CANDY.

One cup of sugar, one-third cup of water. Do not stir while boiling. Boil to amber color; stir in one-fourth teaspoonful cream tartar just before taking from the fire. Wash the figs, open and lay in tin plates and pour the candy over them.

COCOANUT CAKES.

Two cups sugar; half cup water; boil without stirring until crisp when dropped in water; take off fire and beat until it creams; then stir in one grated cocoanut and make into thin cakes.

BOILED FRENCH CREAM CANDY.

One quart sugar, half pint water; stir well together, then do not stir again. Boil ten minutes, then begin to try by dipping fork into it without stirring; if last drop hairs, take a teaspoonful and drop into water, and if you can gather it between finger and thumb in a soft ball it is done. Then pour in shallow dish and let cool. When blood warm begin to stir with spoon; as it stiffens take pieces of it and work between your palms like bread dough; quicker and harder you work the finer your candy; add flavoring. This is the foundation for all French Creams. This cream can be used for Walnut and French Chocolates or Fruit and Nut Creams by following directions given for these varieties in Fruit Creams.

PEPPERMINT DROPS.

Two cups granulated sugar, one-half cup of water; boil five minutes without stirring; flavor quite strong with peppermint; beat until thick. Drop from spoon on well buttered paper.

FLAX SEED CANDY.

One pound of sugar, three-fourths cup of water, one tablespoonful of glycerine, flax seed to suit the taste. Boil sugar, water and glycerine. When nearly done stir in flax seed; pour into buttered pans to cool. Mark into squares.

MARSHMELLOWS.

One half pound white gum arabic, dissolved in pint of water; add one-half pound powdered sugar; place over fire, stir until all is dissolved and of the consistency of honey; gradually add the well beaten whites of four eggs; stir until somewhat thin and does not stick to fingers. Flavor to taste; pour into tin dusted with powdered starch; cut into small squares when cool, and dust with powdered starch.

CAKES.

We have given space to the following Cake recipes, knowing that they will give perfect satisfaction when used with any of the Icings given in this work.

BLACK AND WHITE CAKE.

Two coffee cups of sugar, three-quarters coffee cup of butter, two coffee cups of flour, one coffee cup of milk, one coffee cup of corn starch, two teaspoonfuls baking powder, to one-third batter. For dark cake add one tablespoonful of molasses, one of vinegar, one bowl or cup seeded raisins, spices to make it dark. Bake in three layers, fruit layer in the middle.

VELVET SPONGE CAKE.

Two cups of sugar, one cup boiling water, two and one-half cups flour, six eggs, one teaspoonful baking powder. Beat sugar and eggs. Then add boiling water, then flour. Bake in layers or squares.

MOUNTAIN CAKE.

One cup of butter, two cups of sugar, one cup of milk, four cups of flour, three teaspoonfuls of baking powder, whites of eight eggs. Bake in layers.

FIG CAKE.

One cup of butter, two cups of sugar, four cups of flour, one cup of milk, three teaspoonfuls baking powder, whites of eight eggs. Bake in layers.

DARK.

Three-fourths cup of butter, two cups of sugar, three and one-half cups of flour, one cup of cold water with one teaspoonful soda dissolved in it; yelks of eight eggs, three cups of raisins, chopped fine, one pound of figs sliced, one teaspoonful cinnamon, one teaspoonful nutmeg. Bake in layers; put layers of white then dark. This makes two cakes.

COCOANUT CAKE.

Two cups of sugar, one cup of butter, one cup of milk, four cups of flour, six eggs, two teaspoonfuls baking powder. Bake in layers.

RAILROAD CAKE.

One cup of sugar, one cup of flour, one tablespoonful butter, four tablespoonfuls milk, two eggs; beat ten minutes. Bake in three layers.

COFFEE CAKE.

One cup strong coffee, one cup sugar, one cup molasses, one cup butter, four cups flour, one egg. Bake in layers. Coffee icing.

ALMOND CUSTARD CAKE.

Two cups of sugar, two cups flour, one-half cup of milk, six tablespoonfuls butter, six eggs, one and one-half teaspoonfuls baking powder. Bake in layers and put together with custard.

THE CUSTARD.

One cup of milk, four tablespoonfuls of sugar, three eggs. One pound almonds chopped fine; mix with custard. Almond cream icing.

SPONGE CAKE ROLLS.

Four eggs, one cup of sugar, one cup of flour, one teaspoonful baking powder. Beat eggs and sugar together; add flour and baking powder. Bake in tins 6x10. This makes two rolls. Use any of the French Cream Icing in place of Jelly in these rolls and you will not regret it.

WHIPPED CREAM CAKE.

Four eggs, one cup of sugar, one cup of flour, one teaspoonful baking powder. Bake in three layers. Whip one pint sweet cream; sweeten and flavor to suit taste. Spread between layers. Cream icing on top.

ANGEL CAKE.

Whites of eleven eggs beaten stiff, one and one-half cups of granulated sugar sifted four times, one cup flour sifted twice, two teaspoonfuls cream tartar sifted into the flour. Sift flour, sugar and cream tartar together several times, then sift little at a time into beaten eggs, stirring lightly. Bake in a moderate oven over forty minutes.

HICKORYNUT MACAROONS.

One cup hickorynut meats chopped fine, one cup sugar, one-half cup flour, one egg. Drop on greased paper and bake.

DELICATE CAKE.

One pound of sugar, one pound of flour, one-half pound of butter, whites of fifteen eggs. Rub the butter to a cream, add half the flour; beat the sugar and eggs together, put part of sugar and eggs to flour and butter, then part of flour until all mixed. Flavor to taste. Ice with Cream Frosting.

KISSES.

Whites of four eggs to half pound powdered sugar whipped stiff; flavor to taste. Place upon greased paper and bake same as Cream Meringoes. When done press two of them together.

ORANGE CAKE.

Three cups of sugar, one cup of butter, one-half cup of sour milk, four cups of flour, one grated orange and four eggs; one teaspoonful soda; stir butter and sugar together, add orange and yelks of eggs beaten well, then milk, then flour, last the whites. Squeeze the juice from orange, grate off the yellow rind and do not use the rest of orange.

CORN CAKE.

One cup of butter, two cups of sugar, two cups corn starch, six eggs; beat butter and sugar together, add yelks, then corn starch, and last the well beaten whites. Bake in patty tins in moderate oven.

CUSTARD CAKE.

One cup sugar, one cup flour, four eggs, one teaspoonful baking powder; beat sugar and eggs together thoroughly; add flour; bake in three round layers.

CUSTARD.

One cup of milk, one-half cup of sugar, one egg, one tablespoonful corn starch; wet corn starch with enough milk to work into smooth paste; boil milk; add sugar and egg, then corn starch; stir until smooth and thick. Drop in one-half teaspoonful butter, and when cold flavor to taste; spread between layers; use Fruit Frosting on top.

COCOANUT CAKE.

One pound of cocoanut, one pound of powdered sugar, one-quarter pound of flour, whites of six eggs beaten stiff. Drop on buttered paper and bake in quick oven.

CREAM CAKE.

Four cups of flour, three cups of sugar, two cups of butter, one cup of cream, five eggs, one teaspoonful soda, dissolve in a little milk. Beat butter and sugar to a cream; add yelks, then cream and the soda, then flour and well beaten whites until all mixed. Flavor with lemon Bake in patty tins in quick oven.

BLACK CAKE.

One pound of sugar, one pound of flour, three-fourths of a pound of butter, yelks of twenty eggs, or all of eighteen; two pounds of raisins, two pounds of currants, one pound citron, two teaspoonfuls of cinnamon, two teaspoonfuls of mace, one teaspoonful cloves, one wine glass of brandy.

CREAM MERINGOES

Whites of four eggs whipped stiff, with one pound of powdered sugar; flavor to taste. When very stiff heap in shape of half egg upon greased paper; have them half an inch apart; bake a light brown. When cool spread out the soft inside and fill with whipped cream.

FRUIT CREAM FROSTING.

Rest assured if you follow the instructions you will have a most delicious Frosting.

These Frostings are always right, the making the simplest, and they will remain soft and creamy so as to cut without cracking as long as the cake will keep, and so fine is the quality and flavor that an ordinary cake is made most delicious by this use.

The fruits giving beautiful colors, finest of flavors and the icing remains so creamy as to cut without breaking.

Cold boiled milk, with a teaspoonful glycerine to cup of milk, will answer in place of cream.

PEACH ICING.

Prepare Peach and Cream as for Peach Candy ; stir in confectioners sugar until of the consistency to spread nicely with knife or spatula.

BANANA.

Prepare Banana and Cream as for Banana Candy. Proceed as with Peach Icing.

ORANGE.

Prepare Oranges as for Orange Candy : stir in confectioners sugar until quite stiff ; add two tablespoonfuls cream : stir in sugar until stiff enough to spread with knife or spatula.

PINEAPPLE.

Prepare Pineapple and Cream as for Pineapple Candy. Proceed as for Peach Icing.

GRAPE.

Half cup grape juice ; stir in confectioners sugar until quite stiff ; add two tablespoonfuls sweet cream, rub in sugar until of consistency to spread.

CURRANT.

Half cup currant juice; and proceed as for Orange Icing. White Currants make White Icing and Red Currants a very handsome Pink.

NOTE.

Jellies of any kind or syrup of preserved or canned fruits can be used the same as fresh fruits.

WINE ICING.

Any desired Wine and Cream prepared as for Wine Candy; stir in confectioners sugar until of consistency to spread.

CREAM ICING.

Half cup cream; stir in confectioners sugar until of consistency to spread. Flavor to suit.

CHOCOLATE.

Half cup cream, stir in half cup grated chocolate; rub in confectioners sugar until thick enough to spread.

COCOANUT.

Half cup cream, three-quarters cup grated cocoanut; stir in confectioners sugar to proper consistency; ice cake, and dust or rub grated cocoanut over cake.

FRUIT.

Proceed as for Cream Icing. Add fine chopped raisins, figs, etc., before sugar is all stirred in.

NUT.

Proceed as for Cream Icing. Add fine chopped nuts before sugar is all stirred in.

FIG CREAM FROSTING.

Prepare figs and cream as for Fig Cream Candy No. 1. Stir in confectioners sugar until consistency to spread.

CHOCOLATE CUSTARD.

Grate one-third cake sweet chocolate, one-half cup sweet milk, yelk of one egg, one teaspoonful extract vanilla; sweeten to taste; boil until stiff like jelly; when cold spread between layers.

ICE CREAM FROSTING.

Four cups of powdered sugar, one-half pint water; boil until you can take it in your fingers when dropped in cold water; then pour over the well beaten whites of four eggs, stirring all the time until a perfect cream; add one-half teaspoonful of powdered citric acid and flavor with vanilla, and spread when cold.

BOILED FROSTINGS.

One cup of sugar, a little water; boil until brittle when dropped in cold water; stir quickly into the well beaten white of one egg; add to this one cup of raisins chopped fine or one cup of hickory nut meats, and place between layers and over the top.

SOUPS.

BEEF SOUP.

Cut all the lean off the shank, and with a little beef suet in the bottom of the kettle, fry it to a nice brown; put in the bones and cover with water; cover the kettle closely; let it cook slowly until the meat drops from the bones; strain through a colander and leave it in the dish during the night, which is the only way to get off all the fat. The day it is wanted for the table, fry as brown as possible a carrot, an onion, and a very small turnip sliced thin. Just before taking up, put in half a teaspoonful of sugar, a blade of mace, six cloves, a dozen kernels of allspice, a small teaspoonful of celery seed. With the vegetables this must cook slowly in the soup an hour; then strain again for the table. If you use vermicelli or pearl barley, soak in water.

MUTTON SOUP.

Boil a leg of mutton three hours; season to your taste with salt and pepper, and add one teaspoonful of summer savory; make a batter of one egg, two tablespoons of milk, two tablespoons of flour, all well beaten together; drop this batter into the soup with a spoon and boil for three minutes.

OYSTER SOUP.

Take one quart of water; one teacup of butter; one pint of milk; two teaspoons of salt; four crackers rolled fine, and one teaspoon of pepper; bring to full boiling heat as soon as possible, then add one quart of oysters; let the whole come to boiling heat quickly and remove from the fire.

TOMATO SOUP.

Boil chicken or beef four hours; then strain; add to the soup one can of tomatoes and boil one hour. This will make four quarts of soup.

BEAN SOUP.

One pint beans, four quarts water, small piece fat beef; boil three hours and strain. If too thin add one tablespoon flour.

HOLIDAY BARGAINS

In selecting Christmas Gifts, you can find Reliable Gold and Silver Watches at one-half to three-fourths regular dealers prices, with every usual guarantee on quality; with a fine assortment of Diamonds, Musical Instruments and Jewelry, at corresponding low prices.

These are Unredeemed Pledges that must be turned into Cash by the

OLD AND RELIABLE

HOME SECURITY CO., 149 AT ONTARIO ST.

FINE WATCH REPAIRING A SPECIALTY.

ESTABLISHED 1850.   E. DENISON, PRES.

FISH.

TO BOIL FISH.

Put a small onion inside your fish and tie it up in a towel, cover it with cold water, salt and a little vinegar, and let it heat to the boiling point; from two to three minutes boiling is sufficient for the largest fish, and a small one will not require more than one minute. Fish boiled in this way is incomparably better than when cooked longer.

A SUGGESTION.—Boiling salt water is best for salmon as it sets the color.

BROILED WHITE FISH—FRESH.

Wash and drain the fish; sprinkle with pepper and lay with the inside down upon the gridiron, and broil over fresh bright coals. When a nice brown, turn for a moment on the other side, then take up and spread with butter. This is a very nice way of broiling all kinds of fish, fresh or salted. A little smoke under the fish adds to its flavor. This may be made by putting two or three cobs under the gridiron.

CROQUETTES OF FISH.

Take dressed fish of any kind; separate from the bone, mince it with a little seasoning, an egg beaten with a teaspoon of flour and one of milk; roll into balls, brush the outside with egg and dredge well with bread and cracker crumbs, and fry them of a nice color. The bones, head, tail, an onion, an ancovy and a pint of water will make the gravy.

PANNED OYSTERS.

Drain the oysters from the liquor; put them in a hot pan or spider; as soon as they begin to curl, add butter, pepper and salt. Serve on toast, or without, if preferred.

STEWED OYSTERS.

In all cases, unless shell oysters, wash and drain; mix half a cup of butter and a tablespoon of corn starch; put with the oysters in a porcelain kettle; stir until they boil; add two cups of cream or milk; salt to taste; do not use the liquor of the oysters in either stewing or escaloping.

PURE POP CORN!

You will see by the above letter that the goods I am putting in the market are absolutely pure. If, when buying Pop Corn Fritters, Balls or Sugared Corn, you insist upon getting my goods you will know they are free from impurities.

I am making a specialty of POP CORN, or FAIRY BON-BONS, the finest goods ever made from Pop Corn, made in three flavors, Rose, Vanilla and Maple—very fine for putting in candy bags for Christmas Festivals. Special prices given to Sunday Schools and church fairs.

My Pop Corn Fritters are the finest goods of the kind in the market.

The "Buckeye" brand of Pop Corn for family use, is the best. I use the same corn in these packages that is used in the manufacture of my Fritters.

My goods are sold by all first-class Grocers and Confectioners.

L. A. ANDREWS,

239 VIADUCT.

LEADING
POP CORN
MANUFACTURER

-IN NORTHERN OHIO.

ESCALOPED OYSTERS.

Butter the dish (common earthen pie plates are the best cover the bottom of the dish with very fine bread crumbs; add a layer of oysters; season with pepper and salt; alternate the crumbs and oysters until you have three layers; finish with crumbs; cover the top with small pieces of butter; finish around the edge with bread cut into small oblong pieces dipped in butter; bake half an hour; unless shell oysters, wash them thoroughly and strain.

OYSTER PATTIES.

Stew the oysters; take the broth and allow the yelk of one egg to every dozen of oysters; turn off the broth and add the eggs; let it come to a boi : then turn back the oysters and fill the crust.

POULTRY AND GAME.

ROAST TURKEY OR CHICKEN.

Having picked and drawn the fowls, wash them well in two or three waters; wipe them dry; dredge them with a little flour inside and out, and a little pepper and salt; prepare a dressing of bread and cracker crumbs; fill the bodies and crops of the fowls and then bake them from two to three hours; baste them frequently while roasting; stew the giblets in a sauce pan; just before serving, chop the giblets fine; after taking up the chicken and the water in which the giblets were boiled, add the chopped giblets to the gravy of the roast fowl; thicken with a little flour, which has been previously wet with the water; boil up, and serve in a gravy dish. Roast chickens and turkey should be accompanied with celery and jellies.

BAKED CHICKEN.

Cut the fowls open and lay them flat in a pan, breaking down the breast and the back bones; dredge with flour and season well with salt and pepper, with bits of butter; put into a very hot oven until done, basting frequently with melted butter; or when half done take out the chicken and finish by broiling it upon a gridiron over bright coals; pour over it melted butter and the juices in the pan in which it was baked.

FRIED CHICKEN.

Cut the chicken in pieces, lay it in salt and water, which change several times; roll each piece in flour; fry in very hot lard or butter, season with salt and pepper; fry parsley with them also. Make a gravy of cream seasoned with salt, pepper and a little mace, thickened with a little flour in the pan in which the chickens were fried, pouring off the lard.

CHICKEN PIE.

Boil your chickens until they are tender and season highly, line deep pie plates with a rich crust, take the white meat and a little of the dark off from the bones, put into the pie plates, pour the gravy over the chicken, add butter and a little flour, cover with the crust, bake from half to three-quarters of an hour.

Nautical * * *
⇒Steam⇐
* * * Laundry,

CAPT. C. M. SWARTWOOD, Proprietor.

100 RIVER STREET,

TELEPHONE 2558. CLEVELAND, OHIO.

DRESSING FOR CHICKEN OR TURKEY.

Chop bread crumbs quite fine, season well with pepper, salt and plenty of butter; moisten with a very little water, and add a few oysters with a little of the liquor, if you please. The best authorities say the dressing is the finest when it crumbles as the fowl is cut.

THERE is a tragic list of diseases which women alone may suffer from. Men have their physical distresses, but a man is seldom called upon to endure anything so painful, so lingering, and so tenacious as these diseases to which woman is peculiarly subjected, and which are especially terrible, for the reason that most of them affect the mind as well as the body.

They induce irritability, they destroy ambition, and they injure the memory. Ninety-nine out of a hundred women are afflicted with some of these complaints in a greater or less degree, and so used have they become to pain that they can hardly fancy mortal existence without it. Many of them are women of natural brilliancy, and their possibilities for usefulness would be very great if they were not handicapped by these tormenting troubles.

Women have a way of taking their complaints too much as a matter of course. They say: "Every woman has some trouble. I suppose I ought not to complain." And they thus permit a disease to continue until it absorbs the muscular strength, impoverishes the blood, destroys the beauty, sucks up the mental activity, and leaves the victim a pessimistic, faded inadequate with a hold upon the pity of those about her, but none upon their admiration.

The expense of calling for the treatment of a physician hinders many women from attending to themselves. They do not wish to be an expense to their husbands or fathers, and conceal the suffering until they are almost beyond help. Many young women hesitate to go to a physician because of false modesty. Many have a foolish idea that they will get better after a little while. This is a mistake. The relaxed muscles, the diseased nervous system and the impoverished blood are not likely to get back to their normal condition without aid.

VIAVI is the name of a remedy which cures the diseases to which woman is subject. This statement may well be doubted in the light of almost complete failure with ordinary methods. Still, we may be right. Women who have doctored for many years without success say we are. Others never were well until they used VIAVI. Nearly 100,000 women owe their recovery to VIAVI.

Send 2-cent stamp to the office of the VIAVI CO., No. 11 West Ninth Street, Canton, Ohio, for a 40-page Health Book to Mothers and Daughters. A direct talk, however, is more satisfying. Call during the consultation days, Wednesday and Saturday afternoons, and learn what you may expect from this reform method of treatment.

Every woman bears a great responsibility. She must preserve her own health that she may give a heritage of health to her children. Therefore, let her take her ailments in time. If she does not do so, barrenness, insanity, or a life of terrible physical torment may be her portion. Remember disease is never the will of God. It does not happen. It is caused. Avoid the cause if you can; cure it if you can not.

(COPYRIGHTED.)

MEATS.

ROAST BEEF.

Prepare for the oven by dredging lightly with flour, and seasoning with salt and pepper; place in the oven, and baste frequently while roasting. Allow a quarter of an hour for a pound of meat, if you like it rare; longer if you like it well done. Serve with a sauce, made from the drippings in the pan, to which has been added a tablespoon of Harvey or Worcestershire sauce, and a tablespoon of tomato catsup. Thicken with browned flour and serve in a gravy boat.

MEAT FROM SOUP BONES.

Before thickening the soup or putting in the vegetables, take out a large bowl of the liquor; take the meat from the bones, chop it fine, season with catsup and spices; pour over the liquor, which should be thick enough to jelly when cold; put into moulds and serve cold in slices.

TO BOIL CORNED BEEF.

Put the meat in cold water; boil from five to six hours, then take out the bones; wrap it tightly in a towel; put on ice with a weight to press it.

BOILED TONGUE WITH TOMATO SAUCE.

Half boil a tongue, then stew it with a sauce made of a little broth, flour, parsley, one small onion, one small carrot, salt and pepper, and one can of tomatoes cooked and strained. Lay the tongue on a dish and strain the sauce over it.

BOILED LEG OF MUTTON.

Boil well in clear water until tender, seasoning the water with salt; serve with egg sauce, and garnish with parsley, sliced lemons, or some sour jelly.

TEETH

POSITIVELY FILLED AND
EXTRACTED PAINLESSLY
WITHOUT THE USE OF
VITALIZED AIR OR GAS.

ALL BRANCHES OF

First - Class Dentistry.

TEETH WITHOUT PLATE

AND

GOLD CROWNS A SPECIALTY.

DR. WARRIS,

797 LORAIN ST.,

CORNER FULTON,   TINNERMAN BLOCK.

PRICES REASONABLE.

SOUR PICKLES.

TOMATO CATSUP.

Select good ripe tomatoes, scald and strain through a coarse seive to remove seeds and skins; then add to each gallon when cold, four tablespoons of salt, three of ground mustard, two of black pepper, one of ground allspice, one-half of cloves, one-half of cayenne pepper, and one pint of white wine or cider vinegar; simmer slowly four hours; bottle and cork tight.

PICKLED CABBAGE.

Select solid heads, slice very fine, put in a jar, then cover with boiling water; when cold drain off the water, and season with grated horse radish, salt, equal parts of black and red pepper, cinnamon and cloves whole; cover with strong vinegar. This is convenient and always good.

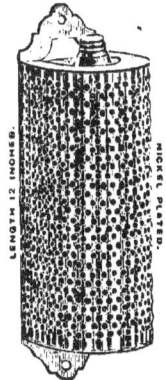

FOR A NICE DELICIOUS LUNCH

USE

SCHULTE'S
Boneless Boiled Ham.

Nothing but the very best Sugar Cured Hams used, and carefully Boiled by Steam Process.

FOR SALE AT ALL FIRST-CLASS

MEAT MARKETS AND GROCERIES.

Special attention given to Balls and Parties.

PREPARED ONLY AT

348 PEARL STREET,

CLEVELAND, OHIO.

PIES.

LEMON PIE.

The rind and juice of one lemon, one cup sugar, the yelk of three eggs; mix these well together; two cups of milk, a little salt, one tablespoon corn starch; thicken the milk with the corn starch and let it come to a boil, then stir it into the other ingredients, pour it into a pie plate covered with a good paste and bake it Beat the whites of three eggs to a froth, with a tablespoon of sugar, lay it over the top of the pie and set it again in the oven for a few seconds to brown.

MINCE MEAT.

Two pounds of raisins, one of currants, one of suet, two and one-half of sugar, one-quarter of citron, one-eighth of cinnamon, two chopped pippins, three lemons, two nutmegs, wine, brandy and cloves to taste.

CUSTARD PIE.

Make a custard of the yelks of three eggs with milk, season to taste; bake it in ordinary crust; put it in a brick oven, that the crust may not be heavy, and as soon as that is heated remove it to a place in the oven of a more moderate heat, that the custard may bake slowly and not curdle; when done, beat the whites to a froth; add sugar and spread over the top, and return to the oven to brown slightly; small pinch of salt added to a custard heightens the flavor; a little soda in the crust prevents it from being heavy.

HEALTH ESSENTIAL TO HAPPINESS.

THERE is no degree of beauty, intelligence or amiability which can compensate for a diseased body in woman. Indeed, there is no beauty, intelligence or amiability which bad health will not undermine. Neither wealth, position nor opportunity can compensate for the absence of health; and the conscientious woman has other reasons than selfish ones, for feeling bad health to be the greatest of misfortunes. She knows that she cannot be ill without casting a shadow over the home that she would, if she could, keep always bright. If she has children, she will not only find herself incapacitated for giving them the mental and moral training they need, but she may not even be able to hold their admiration; and the chances are ten to one that she has given them a hideous heritage of disease. She may well be haunted with the fear that the day will come when they will think of her with contempt, for being willing to bring into the world children who can not escape from the destiny of suffering which her enfeebled constitution bequeathed them. She may well apprehend that the time will come when her husband will weary of coming home to the dim room where the invalid wife is always ailing, and go elsewhere, that he may find the high spirits, the physical vigor, and the entertaining vivacity which he is never able to get in his own home.

In short, however guiltless a woman may be, she cannot but feel that she, a chronic invalid, is daily damaging the lives of those she loves best, and that each day which prolongs her painful and wasted life, is a misfortune rather than a blessing.

Yet, the time never really comes when a woman with anything to live for, is ready to relinquish life, no matter how acute her physical sufferings or how terrible her mental torment.

VIAVI is the name of a remedy which cures the diseases to which woman is subject. This statement may well be doubted in light of almost complete failure with ordinary methods. Still, we may be right. Women who have doctored for many years without success, say we are. Others never were well until they used VIAVI. Nearly 100,000 women owe their recovery to VIAVI.

Send 2 cent stamp to the office of the VIAVI CO., No. 309 "The Nasby," Toledo, Ohio, for 40-page Health Book to Mothers and Daughters. A direct talk, however, is more satisfying. Call during the office hours (1 to 6 p. m.) and learn what you may expect from this reform method of treatment.

Every woman bears a great responsibility. She must preserve her own health that she may give a heritage of health to her children. Therefore, let her take her ailments in time. If she does not do so, barrenness, insanity, or a life of terrible physical torment may be her portion. Remember, disease is never the will of God. It does not happen. It is caused. Avoid the cause if you can; cure it if you can not. (COPYRIGHTED.)

THE SHORT AND POPULAR LINE

www.ingramcontent.com/pod-product-compliance
Lightning Source LLC
Chambersburg PA
CBHW021449090426
42739CB00009B/1692